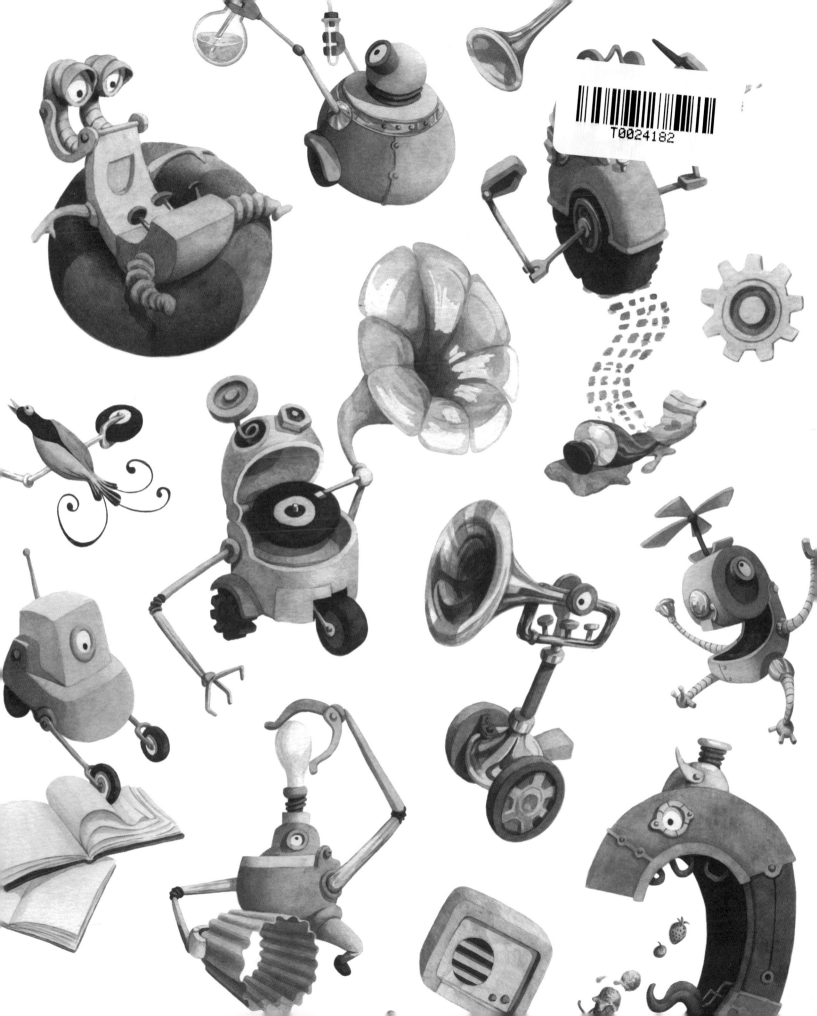

Counting in Dog Years and Other Sassy Math Poems

BETSY FRANCO

ILLUSTRATED BY
PRISCILLA TEY

Candlewick Press

For August, Jack, and Cole
BF

For those who have taught me and
those who continue to teach most earnestly
PT

First edition 2022

Library of Congress Catalog Card Number 2021953339
ISBN 978-1-5362-0116-1

23 24 25 26 27 CCP 10 9 8 7 6 5 4 3

Printed in Shenzhen, Guangdong, China

This book was typeset in Chaparral Pro and Alice.
The illustrations were done in gouache.

Candlewick Press
99 Dover Street
Somerville, Massachusetts 02144

www.candlewick.com

ACKNOWLEDGMENTS

A version of "Math Makes Me Feel Safe" was first published in *Marvelous Math: A Book of Poems*,
compiled by Lee Bennett Hopkins, Simon & Schuster Books for Young Readers, 1997.

A version of "Talented Bees" was first published in *Bees, Snails, and Peacock Tails: Patterns and Shapes . . .
Naturally*, Margaret K. McElderry Books, 2008.

A version of "Moving for Five Minutes Straight" was first published in *The Poetry of Science: The Poetry
Friday Anthology for Science for Kids*, compiled by Sylvia Vardell and Janet Wong, Pomelo Books, 2015.

Contents

HANGING OUT
AT HOME

Multiplying Mice

I know that mice can *multiply*.
  I'm sure 'cause I kept score.
I started out with two of them
  but soon had twenty-four.

I *divided* them in cages.
  Eight cages worked out great.
The mice then *multiplied* again—
  they numbered forty-eight!

My mom said, "I've had quite enough—
  this *doubling* has to stop!"
Then Mom *subtracted* lots of mice
  and sold them to a shop!

To *sum* it up: it's simpler now
  with one cage in the house,
and "Lucky" is the name I gave
  my one remaining mouse!

LUCKY

Eat Your Math

Make fruit kebabs—
melon, grapes.
Form a pattern
with the shapes.

Cut out sugar
cookie dough.
Eighteen stars,
with six per row.

Make some trail mix,
sure to please:
add one cup
of cranberries.

Bright piñata:
Swing, then shout.
Cubes and spheres
come tumbling out.

Ten-cent cups of
lemonade.
Add up all
the profits made.

Nibbled, gobbled,
salty, sweet.
Math can be
a scrumptious treat!

Mom Time

I'll ask a question of my mom—
a *when* or *why* or *who*.
She'll say, "Hold on a minute, hon."
That minute turns to two.

I'll wait around and wait some more.
I'll get my timer set.
Two minutes stretch to . . . five . . . or ten
. . . and still no answer yet!

Today, when she said, "Just a sec,"
I timed my mom . . . and then
one hundred seconds tick-tocked by—
she'd pulled her trick again.

The next time Mom says, "Clean your room.
Right now! Your floor's a wreck!"
I'll answer, "Sure. No problem, Mom.
I'll do it in a sec."

Counting in Dog Years

(Multiply by seven)

My Grandpa Dan is fifty-six.
   His beagle just turned eight.
In doggy years, their ages match.
   Hold on—I'll set you straight.

Since dogs age faster than we do,
   we use a different gauge.
Count seven years per canine year
   to find their human age.

Computing eight times seven makes
   the beagle fifty-six.
The same age as my Grandpa Dan!
   (I'm good at number tricks.)

If Grandpa were a dog, he'd be
   three hundred ninety-two!
I told him that. He laughed and said,
   "I'm glad it isn't true!"

The Stinky Scale

If socks could talk,
mine would yell,
"Wash your feet.
They really smell!"
They'd come unraveled,
flail, and wail,
"Score: 6 on the Stinky Scale!"

THE STINKY SCALE

1. DIRTY HAIR
2. DOGGY BREATH
3. SWEATY PITS
4. LIMBURGER CHEESE
5. LITTER BOX
6. STINKY FEET
7. ROTTEN EGGS
8. OLDY MOLDY BROCCOLI
9. GARBAGE CAN GUTS
10. SKUNK SPRAY

MATH MUSING

Fractions of Me

One fifth of me
is a brother.
One fifth of me
is a son.

One fifth collects
old comic books.
One fifth finds
campouts fun.

One fifth of me
loves shooting hoops
or scoring
a soccer goal.

Five fifths combined
make all of me.
I'm a living,
breathing whole!

How Old Am I?

I'm eight and three-quarters
(right to the day),
which means my ninth birthday
is three months away.
That's twelve complete weeks,
or eighty-four days,
or two thousand sixteen hours away!

Just Wondering

Do numerals get out of sorts?
Do fractions get along?

Do equal signs complain and gripe
when kids get problems wrong?

Do graphs get wiggly
            standing still
            and wish that
            they could play?

Does a million scold its zeroes
for getting in the way?

Does number nine get sick and tired
of being less than ten?
I'd like to be the oldest kid—
every now and then!

14

Washing Machine Magic

The washing machine's a trickster.
   Or else it's a hungry lout.
I put in sixteen dirty socks—
   three-fourths of my socks came out.

What happened to the other four
   that disappeared from sight?
A magic trick, a sleight of hand,
   the washer's appetite?

I think I'll switch to all white socks.
   Then I'll never have a care.
If only half my socks come out,
   I can always make a pair!

Talented Bees

The honeycomb is marvelous.
Look closely and you'll see
a geometric math-terpiece,
thanks to the honeybee.

The bees build cells to form the cone—
each cell's a hexagon.
Those cells share walls on every side.
The shapes go on and on.

The bees were smart to pick a shape
whose sides match to a tee.
In math we say that shapes like that
tessellate perfectly!

SCHOOL
DAZE

Late for School, Again

The squares on the sidewalk are two feet long.
I follow them everywhere.
But they're constantly giving me trouble
when getting from here to there.

It's *five hundred forty-two* sidewalk squares
to get from my house to class.
Those *one thousand eighty-four* feet are why
I'm holding a tardy pass.

My dad always says, "Walk faster to school.
Just shake the fuzz from your head."
But I dislike mornings and "rise and shine."
I'd rather linger in bed.

If only I lived right next to the school,
like this girl in class named Kate.
I'd roll out of bed, walk *forty-two* feet,
and never, ever be late.

Palindromes

Backward or forward,
left or right,
they read exactly the same.

There's Eve and Otto,
Bob and Nan.
Each has a palindrome name.

This also works for
numbers
in a palindro-mania game!

$$11 \times 11 = 121$$
$$111 \times 111 = 12321$$
$$1111 \times 1111 = 1234321$$
$$11111 \times 11111 = 123454321$$
$$111111 \times 111111 = 12345654321$$

Total Time in School

There are twelve months a year,
and some are for school.
The way they're divided
is strictly uncool.

One-fourth is for summer,
three-fourths are for school.
Unbalanced, unfair, and
exceedingly cruel.

That's *three* months of summer
but *nine* months of school!
It must have been grown-ups
who made up
that rule!

Excavating the Lost and Found

We graphed the stuff in Lost and Found
   before they hauled it away.
We spent almost half an hour
   sorting and counting that day.

We lined the water bottles up,
   tossed sweatshirts into a pile.
(I found my favorite hoodie there —
   it was missing for a while.)

We counted jackets, shoes, and toys
   and one cool cowboy hat.
The strangest?
   The pajama top.
We couldn't make sense of that!

Moving for Five Minutes Straight

For thirty seconds,
we stretch our legs,
then lunge
for thirty more.

For sixty seconds,
we pump our arms —
do push-ups
on the floor.

1 MIN=
60 SECONDS

GO!

YOU CAN
DO IT!

For ninety seconds,
it's jumping jacks.
Our teacher claps
the beat.

For ninety seconds,
we run in place —
a burst of
stomping feet.

The second we hear
the whistle blow,
we cheer.
We're glad to stop.

Everyone feels
so tumble-down tired,
wherever we are
we

drop!

ALMOST THERE!

FIVE MINUTES!

World Record Hopscotch

We drew one hundred squares in chalk.
I stepped right up.
I threw my rock.
"I'll try our hopscotch first," I said.
I hopped and jumped
full speed ahead.

At twenty, I was on my way.
At forty, sixty,
still okay.
At eighty, I was bleary-eyed.
By square one hundred,
I was fried.

I turned. I looked. I gasped.
"Oh, no!
Another hundred squares
to go!"

LAST BELL.
SCHOOL'S OUT!

Solids of Summer

A Poem for Two Voices

Voice 1: A solid is
    Voice 2: a 3D shape
        Both: with width and depth and height.

Voice 1: Solids shape
    Voice 2: our summertime,
        Both: when days are sparkly bright.

Voice 1: A cylinder's
    Voice 2: a noodle
        Both: we play with in the pool.

Voice 1: Cubes are formed
    Voice 2: in ice cube trays
        Both: so lemonade stays cool.

Voice 1: A sphere might be
    Voice 2: a baseball
        Both: that soars to clinch a run.

Voice 1: A prism is
    Voice 2: our two-man tent
        Both: for outdoor camping fun.

Voice 1: A cone is filled
    Voice 2: with ice cream
        Both: on a steamy August day.

Voice 1: An octahedron
    Voice 2: is a top
        Both: that spins in games we play.

Voice 1: A truncated
    Voice 2: icosahedron?
        Both: Hey, that's a soccer ball!

Voice 1: It's our very
    Voice 2: favorite solid!
        Both: We just can't wait for fall!

Calling Up Friends to Play

Skye's cell phone number is mostly evens.
  The one with only odds is Steven's.

A pattern emerges when phoning Soo,
  'cause every other digit is 2.

Arash's number has 6-8-4 twice.
  Calling him up sounds like "Three Blind Mice."

In Tanya's number, the 8s dominate.
  I'll call her first since she's *always* late!

Whose number is whose?
Guess the missing digits.

428-63**?**4

748-88**?**8

57**?**-7953

525-2**?**24

684-68**?**9

Hey, Tanya!

Hey, Steven!

Psst! The answers are on the last page!

Arash
00:22

Soo

SKYE

Our First Official Bug Race

We lined them up on the sidewalk
and shouted "Ready . . . go!"
Contestants took a while to move.
The group was very slow.

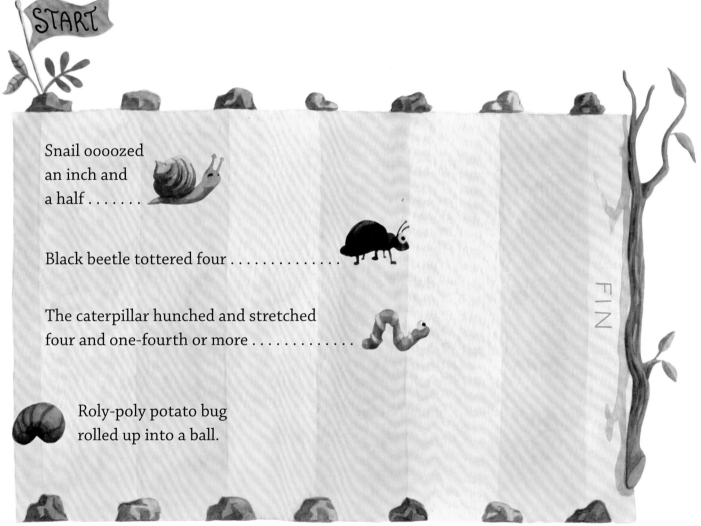

Snail ooooozed
an inch and
a half . . . .

Black beetle tottered four . . . .

The caterpillar hunched and stretched
four and one-fourth or more . . . .

Roly-poly potato bug
rolled up into a ball.

Our First Official Slow-athon
was not a race at all.

Math Makes Me Feel Safe

To some people, math is
just numbers and problems,
but math means a lot more to me.

It's knowing my sister
is seven years younger
(no matter how old I may be).

It's knowing I'll scooter
to school with my neighbor
and get there on time—8:15.

That the holidays come
without fail every year.
(My favorite is still Halloween!)

It's knowing how awesome
Dad's buttermilk pancakes
with syrup and berries will be

(as long as we follow
the recipe closely
and measure things accurately).

34

It's knowing my brother
will help me with drumming
at least twenty minutes each day.

That Saturday-Sunday
comes after each Friday,
and friends will come over to play.

It's knowing that snowflakes—
those six-pointed star shapes—
will dazzle me all winter long.

That the little brown wren
strings notes in a pattern
and starts every day with a song.

It's knowing when night falls
and darkens my bedroom,
my pup sleeps just two feet from me.

That watching stars flicker
in the velvety sky
is my glimpse of infinity!

Calling Up Friends to Play
ANSWER KEY

Skye	**Tanya**	**Steven**	**Soo**	**Arash**
428-63**?**4	748-88**?**8	57**?**-7953	525-2**?**24	684-68**4**9
*(filling in the blank with **any** number works)*	*(filling in **any** number works here, too)*	*(filling in any **odd** number works)*	*(filling in **any** number works here)*